Dinner for Two: 50 Romantic Recipes

By: Kelly Johnson

Table of Contents

- Lobster Tail with Garlic Butter
- Filet Mignon with Red Wine Sauce
- Shrimp Scampi
- Pan-Seared Duck Breast with Cherry Sauce
- Grilled Ribeye Steaks with Herb Butter
- Creamy Tuscan Chicken
- Beef Wellington for Two
- Lemon Garlic Salmon
- Risotto with Asparagus and Parmesan
- Baked Sea Bass with Lemon and Thyme
- Eggplant Parmesan
- Chicken Marsala
- Seared Scallops with Lemon Butter
- Grilled Lamb Chops with Mint Yogurt Sauce
- Pappardelle with Creamy Mushroom Sauce
- Stuffed Chicken Breast with Spinach and Cheese
- Shrimp and Lobster Alfredo
- Caprese Salad with Balsamic Glaze
- Roasted Rack of Lamb
- Sweet Potato Gnocchi with Brown Butter
- Spinach and Ricotta Stuffed Manicotti
- Grilled Shrimp Tacos with Mango Salsa
- Spaghetti Aglio e Olio
- Baked Brie with Fig Jam and Walnuts
- Chicken Piccata
- Blackened Tuna Steaks
- Vegetarian Stuffed Bell Peppers
- Grilled Filet Mignon with Garlic Mashed Potatoes
- Pan-Seared Salmon with Dill Cream Sauce
- Lobster Mac and Cheese
- Roasted Chicken with Garlic and Herbs
- Grilled Veggie Platter with Quinoa
- Beef and Vegetable Stir-Fry
- Pan-Seared Duck with Sweet Potato Puree
- Seared Ahi Tuna with Sesame Crust

- Lemon Herb Grilled Chicken
- Gnocchi with Sage Butter
- Broiled Halibut with Mango Salsa
- Roasted Beet Salad with Goat Cheese
- Braised Short Ribs with Mashed Potatoes
- Stuffed Pork Tenderloin with Apples and Sage
- Creamy Spinach and Ricotta Stuffed Chicken
- Duck Confit with Caramelized Onions
- Grilled Vegetable and Quinoa Salad
- Braised Lamb Shanks
- Prawn and Chorizo Paella
- Lobster Ravioli in a Lemon Cream Sauce
- Grilled Vegetable Kebabs with Tzatziki
- Mushroom and Truffle Oil Risotto
- Chocolate Fondue with Fresh Berries

Lobster Tail with Garlic Butter

Ingredients:

- 2 lobster tails
- 4 tablespoons unsalted butter
- 3 cloves garlic, minced
- 1 tablespoon lemon juice
- 1 tablespoon parsley, chopped
- Salt and pepper to taste
- Lemon wedges for garnish

Instructions:

1. Preheat the oven to 425°F (220°C).
2. Cut the lobster tails down the middle using kitchen scissors, exposing the meat. Gently pull the meat out and place it on top of the shell.
3. In a small saucepan, melt the butter and sauté the garlic for 1-2 minutes until fragrant. Add lemon juice, parsley, salt, and pepper.
4. Brush the lobster meat with the garlic butter mixture, making sure to coat evenly.
5. Bake the lobster tails for 12-15 minutes until the meat is opaque and cooked through.
6. Serve with lemon wedges and additional garlic butter on the side.

Filet Mignon with Red Wine Sauce

Ingredients:

- 2 filet mignon steaks (6-8 oz each)
- 1 tablespoon olive oil
- Salt and pepper to taste
- 1/2 cup red wine
- 1/2 cup beef broth
- 2 tablespoons unsalted butter
- 1 small shallot, minced
- 1 sprig rosemary (optional)

Instructions:

1. Preheat the oven to 400°F (200°C).
2. Season the filet mignon steaks with salt and pepper. Heat olive oil in a skillet over medium-high heat. Sear the steaks for 2-3 minutes on each side until browned.
3. Transfer the skillet to the preheated oven and roast for 5-7 minutes for medium-rare (adjust cooking time for desired doneness).
4. In the same skillet, add the shallots and sauté until soft, about 2 minutes.
5. Pour in the red wine, scraping up any bits from the bottom of the pan. Let it reduce by half, then add the beef broth and rosemary.
6. Simmer the sauce for 5-6 minutes, then whisk in the butter until smooth.
7. Serve the steaks with the red wine sauce poured over the top.

Shrimp Scampi

Ingredients:

- 1 lb large shrimp, peeled and deveined
- 3 tablespoons unsalted butter
- 3 tablespoons olive oil
- 5 cloves garlic, minced
- 1/2 teaspoon red pepper flakes (optional)
- 1/2 cup white wine
- 1 tablespoon lemon juice
- Salt and pepper to taste
- Fresh parsley, chopped
- 8 oz linguine or spaghetti

Instructions:

1. Cook the pasta according to package instructions, then drain, reserving 1/2 cup of pasta water.
2. Heat olive oil and butter in a large skillet over medium heat. Add the garlic and red pepper flakes (if using) and sauté for 1-2 minutes until fragrant.
3. Add the shrimp to the skillet and cook for 2-3 minutes on each side until they turn pink and opaque.
4. Pour in the white wine and lemon juice, stirring to combine. Let the sauce simmer for 2-3 minutes, adding reserved pasta water as needed to thin the sauce.
5. Toss the cooked pasta in the sauce and shrimp mixture. Season with salt, pepper, and chopped parsley before serving.

Pan-Seared Duck Breast with Cherry Sauce

Ingredients:

- 2 duck breasts
- Salt and pepper to taste
- 1 tablespoon olive oil
- 1/2 cup chicken broth
- 1/2 cup red wine
- 1/4 cup fresh cherries, pitted and halved
- 1 tablespoon balsamic vinegar
- 2 tablespoons honey
- 1 tablespoon butter

Instructions:

1. Preheat the oven to 400°F (200°C).
2. Score the skin of the duck breasts in a crisscross pattern, being careful not to cut into the meat. Season with salt and pepper.
3. Heat olive oil in a skillet over medium-high heat. Place the duck breasts skin-side down and sear for 5-7 minutes until the skin is crispy.
4. Flip the duck and transfer the skillet to the oven. Roast for 5-7 minutes for medium-rare.
5. Remove the duck and rest it on a plate. For the sauce, add chicken broth, red wine, cherries, balsamic vinegar, and honey to the skillet. Simmer for 5-7 minutes until the sauce thickens.
6. Stir in butter to finish the sauce. Serve the duck breasts with the cherry sauce poured over them.

Grilled Ribeye Steaks with Herb Butter

Ingredients:

- 2 ribeye steaks (1-inch thick)
- Salt and pepper to taste
- 4 tablespoons unsalted butter, softened
- 1 tablespoon fresh parsley, chopped
- 1 tablespoon fresh thyme, chopped
- 1 teaspoon garlic, minced

Instructions:

1. Preheat the grill to medium-high heat.
2. Season the ribeye steaks with salt and pepper on both sides.
3. Grill the steaks for 4-5 minutes per side for medium-rare (adjust for your desired doneness).
4. While the steaks are grilling, mix the softened butter with parsley, thyme, and garlic.
5. Let the steaks rest for 5 minutes after grilling, then top with herb butter before serving.

Creamy Tuscan Chicken

Ingredients:

- 4 chicken breasts
- Salt and pepper to taste
- 2 tablespoons olive oil
- 1/2 cup sun-dried tomatoes, chopped
- 1/2 cup heavy cream
- 1/4 cup chicken broth
- 2 tablespoons parmesan cheese
- 1 tablespoon fresh basil, chopped
- 2 cups spinach, wilted

Instructions:

1. Season the chicken breasts with salt and pepper. Heat olive oil in a skillet over medium heat.
2. Cook the chicken breasts for 6-7 minutes per side until browned and cooked through. Remove the chicken and set it aside.
3. In the same skillet, add sun-dried tomatoes, heavy cream, chicken broth, and parmesan cheese. Stir to combine and simmer for 5 minutes.
4. Add spinach and cook until wilted. Return the chicken to the skillet and coat it in the creamy sauce.
5. Garnish with fresh basil before serving.

Beef Wellington for Two

Ingredients:

- 2 filet mignon steaks
- Salt and pepper to taste
- 2 tablespoons olive oil
- 4 oz cremini mushrooms, finely chopped
- 1 tablespoon fresh thyme, chopped
- 2 tablespoons Dijon mustard
- 8 oz puff pastry
- 1 egg, beaten

Instructions:

1. Preheat the oven to 400°F (200°C).
2. Season the filet mignon steaks with salt and pepper. Sear in a hot skillet with olive oil for 2-3 minutes per side. Remove from the skillet and brush with Dijon mustard.
3. In the same skillet, cook mushrooms and thyme for 5-6 minutes until the mushrooms release their moisture and become dry.
4. Roll out the puff pastry and place the mushroom mixture in the center. Lay the steaks on top and wrap the pastry around them, sealing the edges.
5. Brush the pastry with the beaten egg and bake for 25-30 minutes, or until golden brown. Let rest before slicing.

Lemon Garlic Salmon

Ingredients:

- 2 salmon fillets
- 1 tablespoon olive oil
- 2 cloves garlic, minced
- 1 tablespoon lemon juice
- Zest of 1 lemon
- Salt and pepper to taste
- Fresh dill for garnish

Instructions:

1. Preheat the oven to 375°F (190°C).
2. Season the salmon fillets with salt, pepper, and lemon zest.
3. Heat olive oil in a skillet over medium heat. Sauté garlic for 1 minute until fragrant.
4. Place the salmon fillets in the skillet, skin-side down, and cook for 2-3 minutes per side. Then transfer the skillet to the oven and bake for 8-10 minutes until the salmon is fully cooked.
5. Drizzle with lemon juice and garnish with fresh dill before serving.

Risotto with Asparagus and Parmesan

Ingredients:

- 1 cup Arborio rice
- 1 tablespoon olive oil
- 1 small onion, finely chopped
- 2 cloves garlic, minced
- 4 cups chicken or vegetable broth, warmed
- 1/2 cup dry white wine
- 1/2 cup parmesan cheese, grated
- 1 bunch asparagus, trimmed and cut into 2-inch pieces
- Salt and pepper to taste

Instructions:

1. Heat olive oil in a large saucepan over medium heat. Add onion and garlic, cooking until soft, about 5 minutes.
2. Add the Arborio rice and cook, stirring for 1-2 minutes.
3. Add wine and cook until mostly absorbed.
4. Gradually add the warmed broth, one ladle at a time, stirring constantly, until the rice is tender (about 18-20 minutes).
5. In a separate skillet, cook the asparagus in a little olive oil for 3-4 minutes until tender.
6. Stir the cooked asparagus into the risotto along with parmesan cheese. Season with salt and pepper, then serve.

Baked Sea Bass with Lemon and Thyme

Ingredients:

- 2 sea bass fillets
- 1 tablespoon olive oil
- 2 cloves garlic, minced
- 1 lemon (sliced into rounds)
- 1 sprig fresh thyme
- Salt and pepper to taste

Instructions:

1. Preheat the oven to 375°F (190°C).
2. Place the sea bass fillets on a baking sheet lined with parchment paper.
3. Drizzle olive oil over the fish and season with salt and pepper.
4. Arrange lemon slices on top of the fillets and sprinkle with minced garlic.
5. Place thyme sprigs on top of the fish.
6. Bake for 15-20 minutes until the fish is cooked through and flakes easily with a fork.
7. Serve with additional lemon wedges for garnish.

Eggplant Parmesan

Ingredients:

- 2 large eggplants, sliced into 1/4-inch rounds
- 1 cup all-purpose flour
- 2 eggs, beaten
- 2 cups breadcrumbs (preferably Italian-style)
- 2 cups marinara sauce
- 2 cups shredded mozzarella cheese
- 1/2 cup grated Parmesan cheese
- 2 tablespoons fresh basil, chopped
- Olive oil for frying

Instructions:

1. Preheat the oven to 375°F (190°C).
2. Season the eggplant slices with salt and let them sit for 15 minutes to draw out excess moisture. Pat dry with paper towels.
3. Dredge each eggplant slice in flour, dip in beaten eggs, and coat in breadcrumbs.
4. Heat olive oil in a skillet over medium heat. Fry the eggplant slices in batches until golden and crispy, about 3-4 minutes per side.
5. In a baking dish, layer the fried eggplant slices, marinara sauce, mozzarella, and Parmesan.
6. Repeat layers until all ingredients are used, finishing with a layer of cheese on top.
7. Bake for 25-30 minutes until the cheese is bubbly and golden. Garnish with fresh basil before serving.

Chicken Marsala

Ingredients:

- 4 boneless, skinless chicken breasts
- Salt and pepper to taste
- 1/2 cup all-purpose flour
- 2 tablespoons olive oil
- 8 oz cremini mushrooms, sliced
- 3/4 cup Marsala wine
- 1/2 cup chicken broth
- 2 tablespoons unsalted butter
- 2 tablespoons fresh parsley, chopped

Instructions:

1. Season the chicken breasts with salt and pepper. Dredge in flour, shaking off any excess.
2. Heat olive oil in a large skillet over medium-high heat. Cook the chicken breasts for 4-5 minutes per side until golden and cooked through. Remove and set aside.
3. In the same skillet, add the mushrooms and cook until soft, about 5 minutes.
4. Pour in the Marsala wine and chicken broth, scraping up any browned bits from the bottom of the skillet.
5. Let the sauce simmer for 5-7 minutes until it reduces by half. Stir in butter until melted.
6. Return the chicken to the skillet, spoon the sauce over the chicken, and cook for an additional 3-4 minutes.
7. Garnish with fresh parsley before serving.

Seared Scallops with Lemon Butter

Ingredients:

- 12 large sea scallops, patted dry
- Salt and pepper to taste
- 2 tablespoons olive oil
- 4 tablespoons unsalted butter
- 2 cloves garlic, minced
- 1 tablespoon lemon juice
- 1 teaspoon lemon zest
- Fresh parsley for garnish

Instructions:

1. Season the scallops with salt and pepper on both sides.
2. Heat olive oil in a skillet over high heat. Once hot, add the scallops and sear for 2-3 minutes on each side until golden brown and opaque.
3. Remove the scallops from the skillet and set aside.
4. In the same skillet, melt the butter over medium heat. Add garlic and sauté for 1 minute until fragrant.
5. Stir in lemon juice and zest, and cook for an additional 1-2 minutes.
6. Return the scallops to the skillet and toss them gently in the lemon butter sauce.
7. Garnish with fresh parsley before serving.

Grilled Lamb Chops with Mint Yogurt Sauce

Ingredients:

- 8 lamb chops
- 2 tablespoons olive oil
- 2 cloves garlic, minced
- 1 tablespoon fresh rosemary, chopped
- Salt and pepper to taste
- 1 cup plain Greek yogurt
- 2 tablespoons fresh mint, chopped
- 1 tablespoon lemon juice
- 1 teaspoon honey

Instructions:

1. Preheat the grill to medium-high heat.
2. Season the lamb chops with olive oil, garlic, rosemary, salt, and pepper. Let marinate for at least 30 minutes.
3. Grill the lamb chops for 4-5 minutes per side for medium-rare (adjust for desired doneness).
4. While the lamb is grilling, mix the yogurt, mint, lemon juice, and honey in a small bowl. Season with salt and pepper.
5. Serve the grilled lamb chops with the mint yogurt sauce on the side.

Pappardelle with Creamy Mushroom Sauce

Ingredients:

- 12 oz pappardelle pasta
- 2 tablespoons olive oil
- 1 small onion, finely chopped
- 2 cloves garlic, minced
- 8 oz mushrooms, sliced
- 1/2 cup heavy cream
- 1/2 cup Parmesan cheese, grated
- Salt and pepper to taste
- Fresh parsley for garnish

Instructions:

1. Cook the pappardelle according to package instructions. Drain, reserving 1/2 cup of pasta water.
2. In a large skillet, heat olive oil over medium heat. Add the onion and garlic, cooking until soft, about 3 minutes.
3. Add the mushrooms and cook for 5-7 minutes until browned and tender.
4. Stir in the heavy cream and Parmesan cheese, cooking until the sauce thickens, about 3 minutes.
5. Toss the cooked pasta in the sauce, adding reserved pasta water as needed to reach the desired consistency.
6. Season with salt and pepper, and garnish with fresh parsley before serving.

Stuffed Chicken Breast with Spinach and Cheese

Ingredients:

- 4 boneless, skinless chicken breasts
- 1 tablespoon olive oil
- 2 cups spinach, wilted
- 1 cup ricotta cheese
- 1/2 cup mozzarella cheese, shredded
- Salt and pepper to taste
- 1/4 cup Parmesan cheese, grated
- 1/4 cup breadcrumbs

Instructions:

1. Preheat the oven to 375°F (190°C).
2. Season the chicken breasts with salt and pepper. Cut a pocket into each breast.
3. In a bowl, mix the spinach, ricotta, mozzarella, Parmesan, and breadcrumbs. Stuff each chicken breast with the mixture.
4. Heat olive oil in a skillet over medium-high heat. Brown the chicken breasts for 3-4 minutes per side.
5. Transfer the chicken to the oven and bake for 20-25 minutes until cooked through.
6. Serve the stuffed chicken breasts with a side of your choice.

Shrimp and Lobster Alfredo

Ingredients:

- 8 oz fettuccine pasta
- 1 tablespoon olive oil
- 1/2 lb shrimp, peeled and deveined
- 1/2 lb lobster tail, chopped
- 3/4 cup heavy cream
- 1/2 cup Parmesan cheese, grated
- 2 cloves garlic, minced
- Salt and pepper to taste
- Fresh parsley for garnish

Instructions:

1. Cook the fettuccine pasta according to package instructions, then drain.
2. Heat olive oil in a large skillet over medium heat. Add shrimp and lobster, cooking until pink and opaque, about 4-5 minutes.
3. Add garlic and sauté for 1 minute until fragrant.
4. Pour in the heavy cream, bringing it to a simmer. Stir in Parmesan cheese and cook until the sauce thickens, about 3-4 minutes.
5. Toss the cooked pasta in the sauce, and season with salt and pepper.
6. Garnish with fresh parsley before serving.

Caprese Salad with Balsamic Glaze

Ingredients:

- 4 ripe tomatoes, sliced
- 1 ball fresh mozzarella, sliced
- Fresh basil leaves
- 2 tablespoons extra virgin olive oil
- 1/4 cup balsamic glaze
- Salt and pepper to taste

Instructions:

1. Arrange the tomato and mozzarella slices alternately on a serving platter.
2. Tuck fresh basil leaves between the slices.
3. Drizzle with olive oil and balsamic glaze.
4. Season with salt and pepper.
5. Serve immediately as a refreshing appetizer or side dish.

Roasted Rack of Lamb

Ingredients:

- 1 rack of lamb (about 8 ribs)
- 2 tablespoons olive oil
- 4 cloves garlic, minced
- 1 tablespoon fresh rosemary, chopped
- 1 tablespoon fresh thyme, chopped
- Salt and pepper to taste
- 1/2 cup red wine (optional)

Instructions:

1. Preheat the oven to 400°F (200°C).
2. Rub the lamb with olive oil, garlic, rosemary, thyme, salt, and pepper.
3. Place the lamb on a roasting rack and roast for 20-25 minutes for medium-rare (adjust for desired doneness).
4. Let the lamb rest for 10 minutes before slicing between the ribs.
5. If desired, deglaze the pan with red wine to make a quick sauce.
6. Serve with your favorite sides for a festive and flavorful main course.

Sweet Potato Gnocchi with Brown Butter

Ingredients:

- 2 cups mashed sweet potatoes
- 1 egg
- 2 cups all-purpose flour
- 1/4 teaspoon nutmeg
- Salt and pepper to taste
- 1/2 cup unsalted butter
- 2 tablespoons fresh sage, chopped
- Parmesan cheese, for serving

Instructions:

1. In a large bowl, mix mashed sweet potatoes, egg, flour, nutmeg, salt, and pepper until a dough forms.
2. Roll the dough into long ropes, then cut into 1-inch pieces and shape with a fork.
3. Bring a large pot of salted water to a boil. Cook the gnocchi in batches until they float to the surface, about 2-3 minutes. Remove with a slotted spoon.
4. In a separate skillet, melt butter over medium heat. Add sage and cook until the butter turns golden brown and fragrant.
5. Toss the cooked gnocchi in the brown butter and serve with Parmesan cheese.

Spinach and Ricotta Stuffed Manicotti

Ingredients:

- 12 manicotti shells
- 2 cups ricotta cheese
- 1 cup cooked spinach, squeezed dry
- 1 egg
- 1/4 teaspoon garlic powder
- 2 cups marinara sauce
- 1 1/2 cups shredded mozzarella cheese
- 1/4 cup grated Parmesan cheese
- Salt and pepper to taste

Instructions:

1. Preheat the oven to 375°F (190°C).
2. Cook the manicotti shells according to package instructions. Drain and set aside.
3. In a bowl, combine ricotta, spinach, egg, garlic powder, salt, and pepper.
4. Stuff the cooked shells with the ricotta mixture and place them in a baking dish.
5. Pour marinara sauce over the stuffed shells and top with mozzarella and Parmesan.
6. Cover with foil and bake for 25 minutes, then uncover and bake for an additional 10 minutes until the cheese is bubbly.
7. Serve hot with extra Parmesan on top.

Grilled Shrimp Tacos with Mango Salsa

Ingredients:

- 1 lb large shrimp, peeled and deveined
- 1 tablespoon olive oil
- 1 tablespoon lime juice
- 1/2 teaspoon chili powder
- Salt and pepper to taste
- 8 small corn tortillas
- 1 mango, diced
- 1/4 cup red onion, diced
- 1/4 cup fresh cilantro, chopped
- 1 tablespoon lime juice
- 1/2 avocado, sliced

Instructions:

1. Preheat the grill to medium-high heat.
2. Toss shrimp in olive oil, lime juice, chili powder, salt, and pepper. Grill the shrimp for 2-3 minutes per side until pink and cooked through.
3. While the shrimp cook, combine mango, red onion, cilantro, and lime juice in a bowl to make the salsa.
4. Warm the tortillas on the grill for 30 seconds per side.
5. Assemble the tacos by placing shrimp on the tortillas, topping with mango salsa and avocado slices.
6. Serve with extra lime wedges for garnish.

Spaghetti Aglio e Olio

Ingredients:

- 12 oz spaghetti
- 1/4 cup olive oil
- 6 cloves garlic, thinly sliced
- 1/4 teaspoon red pepper flakes
- Salt and pepper to taste
- 1/4 cup fresh parsley, chopped
- Grated Parmesan cheese for serving

Instructions:

1. Cook the spaghetti according to package instructions until al dente. Reserve 1/2 cup of pasta water and drain the rest.
2. Heat olive oil in a large skillet over medium heat. Add garlic and cook until golden brown, about 2 minutes.
3. Add the red pepper flakes and toss for another 30 seconds.
4. Add the cooked pasta to the skillet, along with the reserved pasta water. Toss to combine, adding salt and pepper to taste.
5. Garnish with fresh parsley and Parmesan cheese before serving.

Baked Brie with Fig Jam and Walnuts

Ingredients:

- 1 wheel of Brie cheese (8 oz)
- 1/4 cup fig jam
- 1/4 cup walnuts, chopped
- 1 tablespoon honey
- Fresh thyme for garnish
- Crackers or baguette slices for serving

Instructions:

1. Preheat the oven to 350°F (175°C).
2. Place the Brie on a parchment-lined baking sheet and bake for 10-15 minutes until the cheese is soft and gooey.
3. In a small saucepan, heat the fig jam over low heat until warm.
4. Remove the Brie from the oven and top with warm fig jam, chopped walnuts, and a drizzle of honey.
5. Garnish with fresh thyme and serve with crackers or baguette slices.

Chicken Piccata

Ingredients:

- 4 boneless, skinless chicken breasts
- Salt and pepper to taste
- 1/2 cup all-purpose flour
- 3 tablespoons olive oil
- 1/2 cup chicken broth
- 1/4 cup fresh lemon juice
- 1/4 cup capers, drained
- 2 tablespoons unsalted butter
- Fresh parsley for garnish

Instructions:

1. Season the chicken breasts with salt and pepper, then dredge in flour, shaking off any excess.
2. Heat olive oil in a large skillet over medium-high heat. Cook the chicken for 4-5 minutes per side until golden brown and cooked through. Remove the chicken from the skillet.
3. Add chicken broth and lemon juice to the skillet, scraping up any browned bits. Bring to a simmer and cook for 2-3 minutes.
4. Stir in capers and butter, cooking until the butter melts.
5. Return the chicken to the skillet, spoon the sauce over the chicken, and cook for an additional 2 minutes.
6. Garnish with fresh parsley before serving.

Blackened Tuna Steaks

Ingredients:

- 4 tuna steaks (6 oz each)
- 2 tablespoons olive oil
- 1 tablespoon paprika
- 1/2 teaspoon cayenne pepper
- 1 teaspoon garlic powder
- 1/2 teaspoon onion powder
- Salt and black pepper to taste
- Fresh lemon wedges for serving

Instructions:

1. In a small bowl, combine paprika, cayenne pepper, garlic powder, onion powder, salt, and black pepper.
2. Rub the tuna steaks with olive oil and coat with the spice mixture.
3. Heat a skillet over high heat and sear the tuna steaks for 2-3 minutes per side for medium-rare (adjust for desired doneness).
4. Remove the tuna from the skillet and let rest for a few minutes before slicing.
5. Serve with fresh lemon wedges for garnish.

Vegetarian Stuffed Bell Peppers

Ingredients:

- 4 large bell peppers (any color)
- 1 cup cooked quinoa
- 1 can black beans, drained and rinsed
- 1 cup corn kernels
- 1/2 cup diced tomatoes
- 1/2 cup shredded cheddar cheese (optional)
- 1 teaspoon cumin
- 1/2 teaspoon chili powder
- Salt and pepper to taste
- Fresh cilantro for garnish

Instructions:

1. Preheat the oven to 375°F (190°C).
2. Cut the tops off the bell peppers and remove the seeds and membranes.
3. In a large bowl, combine quinoa, black beans, corn, diced tomatoes, cumin, chili powder, salt, and pepper.
4. Stuff the peppers with the quinoa mixture and place them in a baking dish.
5. Top with shredded cheese (if using) and cover with foil.
6. Bake for 25 minutes, then remove the foil and bake for another 5 minutes until the peppers are tender and the cheese is melted.
7. Garnish with fresh cilantro before serving.

Grilled Filet Mignon with Garlic Mashed Potatoes

Ingredients:

- 4 filet mignon steaks
- Salt and pepper to taste
- 2 tablespoons olive oil
- 4 cloves garlic, minced
- 4 medium potatoes, peeled and cubed
- 1/4 cup heavy cream
- 2 tablespoons unsalted butter

Instructions:

1. Preheat your grill to medium-high heat.
2. Season the filet mignon steaks with salt and pepper, then rub with olive oil.
3. Grill the steaks for 4-5 minutes per side for medium-rare, or longer for your preferred doneness.
4. Meanwhile, place the potatoes in a pot of salted water and bring to a boil. Cook for 15-20 minutes, or until tender.
5. Drain the potatoes and return them to the pot. Mash with garlic, heavy cream, and butter until smooth.
6. Serve the grilled filet mignon with a side of creamy garlic mashed potatoes.

Pan-Seared Salmon with Dill Cream Sauce

Ingredients:

- 4 salmon fillets
- Salt and pepper to taste
- 2 tablespoons olive oil
- 1/2 cup sour cream
- 1 tablespoon Dijon mustard
- 1 tablespoon fresh dill, chopped
- 1 tablespoon lemon juice

Instructions:

1. Season the salmon fillets with salt and pepper.
2. Heat olive oil in a large skillet over medium-high heat. Add the salmon and cook for 4-5 minutes per side, until golden brown and cooked through.
3. In a small bowl, combine sour cream, Dijon mustard, dill, and lemon juice.
4. Serve the salmon fillets with a dollop of dill cream sauce on top.

Lobster Mac and Cheese

Ingredients:

- 2 lobster tails
- 8 oz elbow macaroni
- 2 tablespoons butter
- 2 tablespoons flour
- 1 1/2 cups milk
- 1 1/2 cups shredded sharp cheddar cheese
- 1/2 cup grated Parmesan cheese
- 1/2 teaspoon garlic powder
- Salt and pepper to taste
- Fresh parsley for garnish

Instructions:

1. Cook the macaroni according to package instructions. Drain and set aside.
2. Bring a pot of water to a boil and cook the lobster tails for 5-7 minutes, until fully cooked. Remove the lobster meat and chop into bite-sized pieces.
3. In a saucepan, melt butter over medium heat. Stir in the flour and cook for 1-2 minutes.
4. Slowly whisk in the milk, then cook and stir until the sauce thickens.
5. Stir in the cheddar cheese, Parmesan cheese, garlic powder, salt, and pepper.
6. Combine the cooked macaroni and lobster meat with the cheese sauce. Stir to coat, then garnish with fresh parsley before serving.

Roasted Chicken with Garlic and Herbs

Ingredients:

- 1 whole chicken (about 4 lbs)
- 4 cloves garlic, smashed
- 1 lemon, halved
- 3 tablespoons olive oil
- 2 tablespoons fresh rosemary, chopped
- 2 tablespoons fresh thyme, chopped
- Salt and pepper to taste

Instructions:

1. Preheat the oven to 400°F (200°C).
2. Rub the chicken inside and out with olive oil, then season with salt, pepper, rosemary, and thyme.
3. Stuff the chicken with smashed garlic and lemon halves.
4. Place the chicken on a roasting rack in a baking dish and roast for 1 hour and 15 minutes, or until the internal temperature reaches 165°F (75°C).
5. Let the chicken rest for 10 minutes before carving and serving.

Grilled Veggie Platter with Quinoa

Ingredients:

- 1 zucchini, sliced
- 1 yellow squash, sliced
- 1 red bell pepper, cut into strips
- 1 eggplant, sliced
- 1 cup quinoa
- 2 tablespoons olive oil
- Salt and pepper to taste
- 1 tablespoon balsamic glaze

Instructions:

1. Cook the quinoa according to package instructions and set aside.
2. Preheat the grill to medium-high heat.
3. Toss the sliced vegetables with olive oil, salt, and pepper.
4. Grill the vegetables for 4-5 minutes per side, until tender and charred.
5. Arrange the grilled vegetables on a platter with quinoa and drizzle with balsamic glaze before serving.

Beef and Vegetable Stir-Fry

Ingredients:

- 1 lb beef sirloin, thinly sliced
- 1 red bell pepper, sliced
- 1 yellow onion, sliced
- 2 carrots, julienned
- 1 cup snap peas
- 2 tablespoons soy sauce
- 1 tablespoon hoisin sauce
- 1 tablespoon sesame oil
- 1 teaspoon ginger, grated
- 2 cloves garlic, minced
- Cooked rice for serving

Instructions:

1. Heat sesame oil in a large skillet or wok over medium-high heat.
2. Add the beef and cook until browned, about 3-4 minutes. Remove and set aside.
3. In the same skillet, add garlic, ginger, bell pepper, onion, carrots, and snap peas. Stir-fry for 4-5 minutes, until tender-crisp.
4. Return the beef to the skillet and add soy sauce and hoisin sauce. Stir to combine and cook for an additional 2 minutes.
5. Serve over cooked rice.

Pan-Seared Duck with Sweet Potato Puree

Ingredients:

- 4 duck breasts
- Salt and pepper to taste
- 2 medium sweet potatoes, peeled and cubed
- 2 tablespoons butter
- 1/4 cup heavy cream
- 1/2 teaspoon cinnamon

Instructions:

1. Season the duck breasts with salt and pepper. Score the skin in a crosshatch pattern.
2. Heat a skillet over medium-high heat. Place the duck breasts skin-side down and cook for 5-7 minutes until the skin is crispy. Flip the breasts and cook for another 5-6 minutes, until the duck is medium-rare.
3. Meanwhile, cook the sweet potatoes in boiling salted water for 15 minutes, or until tender. Drain and mash with butter, heavy cream, and cinnamon.
4. Serve the duck breasts with a side of sweet potato puree.

Seared Ahi Tuna with Sesame Crust

Ingredients:

- 4 ahi tuna steaks
- 1/4 cup sesame seeds
- 1 tablespoon olive oil
- Salt and pepper to taste
- Soy sauce for dipping
- Wasabi for serving (optional)

Instructions:

1. Season the tuna steaks with salt and pepper, then coat each side with sesame seeds.
2. Heat olive oil in a skillet over medium-high heat. Sear the tuna steaks for 1-2 minutes per side for rare, or longer for desired doneness.
3. Serve the tuna with soy sauce and wasabi for dipping.

Lemon Herb Grilled Chicken

Ingredients:

- 4 boneless, skinless chicken breasts
- 2 tablespoons olive oil
- 1 lemon, juiced and zested
- 3 cloves garlic, minced
- 1 tablespoon fresh thyme, chopped
- 1 tablespoon fresh rosemary, chopped
- Salt and pepper to taste

Instructions:

1. In a bowl, combine olive oil, lemon juice, lemon zest, garlic, thyme, rosemary, salt, and pepper.
2. Place the chicken breasts in a resealable bag or shallow dish, pour the marinade over the chicken, and refrigerate for at least 30 minutes, or up to 2 hours.
3. Preheat the grill to medium-high heat.
4. Grill the chicken for 6-7 minutes per side, or until fully cooked and the internal temperature reaches 165°F (75°C).
5. Serve the grilled chicken with a garnish of fresh herbs and lemon wedges.

Gnocchi with Sage Butter

Ingredients:

- 1 lb potato gnocchi
- 1/4 cup unsalted butter
- 10 fresh sage leaves
- 1/4 teaspoon nutmeg
- Salt and pepper to taste
- Fresh Parmesan cheese for serving

Instructions:

1. Cook the gnocchi according to package instructions, then drain and set aside.
2. In a large skillet, melt the butter over medium heat. Add the sage leaves and cook until the butter turns golden brown and the sage becomes crispy, about 3-4 minutes.
3. Add the cooked gnocchi to the skillet, and toss to coat in the butter and sage.
4. Season with salt, pepper, and a pinch of nutmeg.
5. Serve with freshly grated Parmesan cheese.

Broiled Halibut with Mango Salsa

Ingredients:

- 4 halibut fillets
- 2 tablespoons olive oil
- Salt and pepper to taste
- 1 ripe mango, diced
- 1/4 red onion, finely chopped
- 1 small jalapeño, seeded and minced
- 1 tablespoon fresh cilantro, chopped
- 1 tablespoon lime juice

Instructions:

1. Preheat the broiler to high and place an oven rack about 6 inches from the heat source.
2. Drizzle the halibut fillets with olive oil and season with salt and pepper.
3. Place the fillets under the broiler and cook for 4-5 minutes per side, until the fish is opaque and flakes easily with a fork.
4. While the fish is cooking, combine mango, red onion, jalapeño, cilantro, and lime juice in a bowl to make the salsa.
5. Serve the broiled halibut fillets topped with mango salsa.

Roasted Beet Salad with Goat Cheese

Ingredients:

- 4 medium beets, peeled and cut into wedges
- 2 tablespoons olive oil
- Salt and pepper to taste
- 2 cups mixed greens (arugula, spinach, etc.)
- 1/4 cup goat cheese, crumbled
- 1/4 cup walnuts, toasted
- 1 tablespoon balsamic vinegar

Instructions:

1. Preheat the oven to 400°F (200°C).
2. Toss the beet wedges with olive oil, salt, and pepper, and spread them in a single layer on a baking sheet.
3. Roast for 30-35 minutes, flipping halfway through, until the beets are tender.
4. In a bowl, toss the roasted beets with mixed greens, goat cheese, and toasted walnuts.
5. Drizzle with balsamic vinegar and serve.

Braised Short Ribs with Mashed Potatoes

Ingredients:

- 4 bone-in beef short ribs
- Salt and pepper to taste
- 2 tablespoons olive oil
- 1 onion, chopped
- 2 carrots, chopped
- 2 celery stalks, chopped
- 4 cloves garlic, minced
- 1 cup red wine
- 2 cups beef broth
- 1 tablespoon fresh thyme
- 1 bay leaf
- 2 lbs potatoes, peeled and cubed
- 1/4 cup heavy cream
- 2 tablespoons unsalted butter

Instructions:

1. Preheat the oven to 325°F (160°C).
2. Season the short ribs with salt and pepper. Heat olive oil in a large Dutch oven over medium-high heat. Brown the short ribs on all sides, then remove and set aside.
3. Add onion, carrots, celery, and garlic to the Dutch oven and cook for 5-7 minutes, until softened.
4. Pour in the red wine and scrape up any browned bits from the bottom of the pot. Add the beef broth, thyme, and bay leaf, then return the short ribs to the pot.
5. Cover and braise in the oven for 2.5-3 hours, until the meat is tender and falling off the bone.
6. Meanwhile, boil the potatoes in salted water for 15-20 minutes, until tender. Drain and mash with heavy cream and butter.
7. Serve the short ribs with mashed potatoes, spooning some of the braising liquid over the top.

Stuffed Pork Tenderloin with Apples and Sage

Ingredients:

- 2 pork tenderloins (about 1 lb each)
- Salt and pepper to taste
- 2 tablespoons olive oil
- 1 apple, peeled and chopped
- 1/2 onion, finely chopped
- 1/4 cup breadcrumbs
- 1 tablespoon fresh sage, chopped
- 1/4 cup chicken broth

Instructions:

1. Preheat the oven to 375°F (190°C).
2. Season the pork tenderloins with salt and pepper. Using a sharp knife, slice each tenderloin lengthwise to create a pocket.
3. In a skillet, heat olive oil over medium heat. Add the apple, onion, and sage, and sauté for 5-7 minutes, until softened. Stir in the breadcrumbs and cook for another 2 minutes.
4. Stuff the pork tenderloins with the apple mixture, then secure the openings with toothpicks or kitchen twine.
5. Heat a little more olive oil in a skillet and sear the pork on all sides until browned.
6. Transfer the pork to the oven and roast for 25-30 minutes, or until the internal temperature reaches 145°F (63°C).
7. Let the pork rest for 10 minutes before slicing and serving with chicken broth drizzled over the top.

Creamy Spinach and Ricotta Stuffed Chicken

Ingredients:

- 4 boneless, skinless chicken breasts
- Salt and pepper to taste
- 1 cup ricotta cheese
- 1/2 cup cooked spinach, squeezed dry and chopped
- 1/4 cup grated Parmesan cheese
- 2 cloves garlic, minced
- 1 tablespoon olive oil

Instructions:

1. Preheat the oven to 375°F (190°C).
2. Season the chicken breasts with salt and pepper. Using a sharp knife, create a pocket in each chicken breast.
3. In a bowl, mix ricotta cheese, spinach, Parmesan, and garlic until well combined.
4. Stuff each chicken breast with the spinach mixture and secure with toothpicks.
5. Heat olive oil in a skillet over medium-high heat. Sear the chicken breasts on both sides until golden brown, about 3-4 minutes per side.
6. Transfer the chicken to the oven and bake for 20-25 minutes, or until the internal temperature reaches 165°F (75°C).
7. Serve hot.

Duck Confit with Caramelized Onions

Ingredients:

- 4 duck leg quarters
- Salt and pepper to taste
- 4 cups duck fat (or vegetable oil)
- 2 large onions, thinly sliced
- 2 tablespoons balsamic vinegar

Instructions:

1. Season the duck legs with salt and pepper. In a large Dutch oven, melt duck fat over low heat and submerge the duck legs. Cook slowly for 2-3 hours until tender.
2. Remove the duck legs from the fat and set aside.
3. In the same Dutch oven, add onions and cook over medium heat until caramelized, about 15 minutes.
4. Stir in balsamic vinegar and cook for another 2-3 minutes.
5. Serve the duck legs with caramelized onions on top.

Grilled Vegetable and Quinoa Salad

Ingredients:

- 1 cup quinoa
- 2 zucchinis, sliced
- 1 red bell pepper, chopped
- 1 eggplant, chopped
- 1 cup cherry tomatoes, halved
- 2 tablespoons olive oil
- Salt and pepper to taste
- 1 tablespoon fresh basil, chopped
- 1 tablespoon balsamic vinegar

Instructions:

1. Cook the quinoa according to package instructions and set aside.
2. Preheat the grill to medium-high heat. Toss the zucchini, bell pepper, and eggplant with olive oil, salt, and pepper.
3. Grill the vegetables for 3-4 minutes per side, until tender and lightly charred.
4. In a large bowl, toss the quinoa, grilled vegetables, cherry tomatoes, basil, and balsamic vinegar.
5. Serve warm or at room temperature.

Braised Lamb Shanks

Ingredients:

- 4 lamb shanks
- Salt and pepper to taste
- 2 tablespoons olive oil
- 1 onion, chopped
- 2 carrots, chopped
- 2 celery stalks, chopped
- 4 cloves garlic, minced
- 1 cup red wine
- 2 cups beef broth
- 2 sprigs fresh rosemary
- 1 sprig thyme
- 1 bay leaf

Instructions:

1. Preheat the oven to 325°F (160°C).
2. Season the lamb shanks with salt and pepper. Heat olive oil in a large Dutch oven over medium-high heat. Brown the lamb shanks on all sides, then remove and set aside.
3. Add onion, carrots, celery, and garlic to the Dutch oven and cook for 5-7 minutes until softened.
4. Pour in the red wine and scrape up any browned bits from the bottom of the pot. Add the beef broth, rosemary, thyme, and bay leaf.
5. Return the lamb shanks to the pot, cover, and braise in the oven for 2.5-3 hours until the meat is tender and falling off the bone.
6. Remove the lamb shanks from the pot and let them rest for 10 minutes before serving with the braising liquid.

Prawn and Chorizo Paella

Ingredients:

- 1 lb prawns, peeled and deveined
- 1/2 lb chorizo sausage, sliced
- 1 tablespoon olive oil
- 1 onion, chopped
- 1 bell pepper, chopped
- 2 cloves garlic, minced
- 1 1/2 cups Arborio rice (or paella rice)
- 3 cups chicken broth
- 1/2 teaspoon paprika
- 1/4 teaspoon saffron threads (optional)
- Salt and pepper to taste
- 1/2 cup frozen peas
- 2 tablespoons fresh parsley, chopped
- Lemon wedges for serving

Instructions:

1. In a large pan or paella pan, heat olive oil over medium heat. Add the chorizo slices and cook for 3-4 minutes until browned. Remove and set aside.
2. In the same pan, add the onion, bell pepper, and garlic. Cook for 5 minutes until softened.
3. Stir in the rice and cook for 1-2 minutes, allowing the rice to lightly toast.
4. Pour in the chicken broth, paprika, saffron (if using), salt, and pepper. Bring to a simmer and cook for 10-12 minutes without stirring.
5. Add the prawns, chorizo, and peas to the pan. Continue to cook for another 5-7 minutes, or until the prawns are pink and the rice is tender and the liquid has been absorbed.
6. Garnish with parsley and serve with lemon wedges.

Lobster Ravioli in a Lemon Cream Sauce

Ingredients:

- 1 lb lobster ravioli (store-bought or homemade)
- 1/2 cup heavy cream
- 2 tablespoons unsalted butter
- 1/4 cup fresh lemon juice
- 1 teaspoon lemon zest
- Salt and pepper to taste
- Fresh parsley, chopped for garnish
- Grated Parmesan cheese for serving

Instructions:

1. Cook the lobster ravioli according to package instructions, then drain and set aside.
2. In a skillet, melt butter over medium heat. Add the heavy cream, lemon juice, and lemon zest. Stir and cook for 3-4 minutes until the sauce thickens slightly.
3. Season with salt and pepper.
4. Add the cooked ravioli to the skillet and toss gently to coat in the lemon cream sauce.
5. Serve immediately, garnished with parsley and grated Parmesan.

Grilled Vegetable Kebabs with Tzatziki

Ingredients:

- 1 zucchini, sliced
- 1 red bell pepper, chopped into chunks
- 1 yellow bell pepper, chopped into chunks
- 1 red onion, chopped into chunks
- 1 cup cherry tomatoes
- 1 tablespoon olive oil
- Salt and pepper to taste
- 8 skewers (wooden or metal)

For the Tzatziki:

- 1 cup Greek yogurt
- 1 cucumber, grated and drained
- 1 clove garlic, minced
- 1 tablespoon fresh dill, chopped
- 1 tablespoon lemon juice
- Salt and pepper to taste

Instructions:

1. Preheat the grill to medium-high heat.
2. Thread the zucchini, bell peppers, onion, and cherry tomatoes onto the skewers.
3. Drizzle the vegetable kebabs with olive oil and season with salt and pepper.
4. Grill the skewers for 5-7 minutes, turning occasionally, until the vegetables are tender and slightly charred.
5. For the tzatziki, combine Greek yogurt, grated cucumber, garlic, dill, lemon juice, salt, and pepper in a bowl.
6. Serve the grilled vegetable kebabs with a side of tzatziki for dipping.

Mushroom and Truffle Oil Risotto

Ingredients:

- 1 1/2 cups Arborio rice
- 2 tablespoons unsalted butter
- 1 small onion, chopped
- 3 cups vegetable or chicken broth, warm
- 1 cup white wine
- 2 cups mixed mushrooms (e.g., cremini, shiitake, or button), sliced
- 1/4 cup grated Parmesan cheese
- 1 tablespoon truffle oil
- Salt and pepper to taste
- Fresh parsley, chopped for garnish

Instructions:

1. In a large pan, melt butter over medium heat. Add the onion and cook for 5 minutes until softened.
2. Stir in the rice and cook for 1-2 minutes until lightly toasted.
3. Pour in the white wine and cook until absorbed.
4. Gradually add the warm broth, 1/2 cup at a time, stirring frequently until the liquid is absorbed before adding more. Continue until the rice is tender, about 18-20 minutes.
5. Meanwhile, sauté the mushrooms in a separate pan over medium heat for 5-7 minutes until softened and browned.
6. Once the risotto is creamy and the rice is tender, stir in the mushrooms, Parmesan cheese, truffle oil, salt, and pepper.
7. Serve garnished with fresh parsley.

Chocolate Fondue with Fresh Berries

Ingredients:

- 8 oz dark chocolate (70% cocoa), chopped
- 1/2 cup heavy cream
- 1 tablespoon unsalted butter
- 1 teaspoon vanilla extract
- Fresh strawberries, raspberries, blueberries, and other berries for dipping
- Marshmallows, cubed cake, or other dippables (optional)

Instructions:

1. In a heatproof bowl, combine the chopped chocolate, heavy cream, and butter.
2. Place the bowl over a pot of simmering water (double boiler method), stirring until the chocolate is completely melted and smooth.
3. Remove from heat and stir in the vanilla extract.
4. Transfer the chocolate mixture to a fondue pot or serving bowl.
5. Arrange fresh berries and other dippables around the chocolate and serve immediately.